Casino Slot Analysis Simplified

Daniel Hansen

ISBN-13:
978-1514356678

ISBN-10:
1514356678

DEDICATION

Dedicated to my grandmothers Edna Dawson and Josephine Horlacher

CONTENTS

INTRODUCTION

I work in a Temple. A place of hope. A building filled with the comfort of community, friendship, and family. It is a golden land where superstitions breed in their most beautiful forms. I work for the greatest temple in the modern world. Where the oldest religion gets a new look. I know words like greatest are subjective in the spiritual. Can a Catholic really claim their religion is greater than a Hindus? They can and they cannot. In this sense, this preference, I claim that the temples in which I spend my days are the most glorious and most wondrous of all temples.

You laugh. You disagree. You grow angry at my assertion.

But have you felt the full majesty, which is this temple of mine? It is here that old ladies come to mingle with their friends. They gossip and bask in a power greater than their own. They drag their young daughters and old husbands into this sacred space. Communities are formed mixing together of young and old, male and female, rich and poor. Communities that tie their lives with a secret shared value system that stretches out in the rest of their lives. We are the Temple to which they come and share their communion of tickets and coins. We offer light and sparkle. We offer love and friendship.

It is this that few outsiders understand. We use the word guest instead of customer, because a temple is a home not a business. My guests are friends. I know more about their lives than their own children do. I am here for them to come and see every day. I stand with open arms and more important open ears. Their blight is my blight. Like a priest I take their communion and listen to every word. I stand in steed of the son that never calls or the brother who passed away. I care that their dog has passed. I comfort when they are diagnosed with some illness. I care for them as much as any priest who tends his flock. They are mine and I am theirs, because we are merely part of this great place. For it is the Temple of Gold. Known to the greater world as Casinos. The home of the great spirits of Luck and Fate. They are conspiring together to redistribute wealth through chance and a possibility to fulfill one's dreams. We are the sparkling jewel filling the eyes, hearts, and pockets of those around us. All this for the price of a small offering on the altar of Luck.

If you are reading this I hope that you also understand the bonding that occurs amongst players and employees. Personality for a floor worker and management is vital to the casino's ability to really succeed in business. You and your staff will need to be the type of people that really bond and care for strangers. The type of people who can start a conversation with a complete stranger and really care about what is said.

I started working in the Gaming Industry in September of 1997 at a small Native Casino. I have spent my entire adult life learning everything I can about how the industry works. I perform

Slot Analysis and determine game layouts. I plan out floors and

train employees. My first small Native Casino has grown into a

thing of beauty. I was once told to do what you love and work will

be a joy. My life's work has been a joy to me, and I hope to

others. The industry is not easy. It is highly regulated, extremely

political, and downright frustrating at times. But every day is new

and exciting. I wrote a book before this about supervising and my

lessons on it. The book is a bit older now, but still a good starting

point. As I grow older my focus has become less on strict policy

and more on living within the chaos of the crowd. Believing in my

people to create a family. Finding joy in what I do. Concentrating

on keeping my goals, both short term and long term, always

driving my actions.

My employees and co-workers are a family. Having spent

my entire adult life in the casino industry and Indian Country

specifically I have no idea if other industries are built like us. We

spend our entire lives together. I have had a single Christmas off at this writing, so 18 of my last 19 Christmases have been spent with my customers and coworkers. This can be equally said about just about every single holiday other people get off. We work long hard hours together. Most of us hang out outside of work because so few other people keep our schedules. We are a family, and that makes work both a joy and a frustration. I love the people I work with. And yet sometimes I am faced with them not living up to their potential, and that is a frustration. But who among us has the perfect family?

Finding joy in what you do is the best advice I can give anyone. I often listen to other people talk about retirement and long vacations where they do nothing, and it scares me. I am not too proud to admit life without work is a terror. A phobia if you will. I try to imagine myself resting in a hammock somewhere. I shudder and just cannot stomach the thought of it. How could one live a life so stagnate, bored with the humdrum failure of purpose. We need purpose to keep moving, to keep acting, and mine has always been work. My employees keep me going, my goals keep me moving, and my customers keep me hopping. I fear I just do not have enough hobbies to even consider something as silly as retirement.

Loving what you do is a great blessing in life, and I have a hundred stories about what I do. I give out little awards in my head to people for all the amazing things they do. My favorite awards all surround how people choose to obtain their goals. I once was called up to the main cashier's cage in order to handle an angry customer. She had written several bad checks at our establishment. She was angry that we were not going to allow her to cash another. I was a new manager and she reminded me of my grandmother, so I allowed her to stand close to me. Her husband had been a local large city's sheriff. She seemed like a nice enough lady. Excusing her current anger. I explained to her that there was no way I could approve a check when she had two outstanding, but she was free to use our ATMs. She began digging into her purse. I stepped closer smiling using my hand to point the way to the nearest ATM. And without anger, or another word this nice lady maced me. Through burning eyes and shrinking breath, I heard this lady ask, "now where is the other manager, I know he will cash my checks." And she became the first winner of my, "Creative Solutions" award. An award given to those who create the most unusual solutions to their problems (a book unto itself those awards). I am hard pressed to support her choice in methodology in removing me as an obstacle. I can though recognize the sheer audacity of her actions and her willingness to go all in to achieve her goals.

There are a lot of good books about loving what you do, and a lot of good literature about setting and achieving goals. I flip through them, read them, at times study them. And so, I know that in this regards, I probably have little in the lines of new information. But what do I know about? As I said my industry is not all cakes and cookies followed by mommy's hugs. It is highly regulated, extremely political, and downright frustrating at times. What I can write about is first how to perform the job at hand. The slot analysis the supervisory tasks and such. Maybe later, I will tackle how to navigate these regulations and deal with the politics of the job, and hopefully salve some of that frustration.

I have been in the tribal gaming industry since 1997 and in that time I have worked in almost every department and accepted any challenge offered. I am currently a Gaming Executive for a tribal casino, and have been in management for my entire adult life. I have an in-depth understanding of not just upper management, but of each department within a casino. I became a floor manager before we had OTB, a hotel, golf course, a restaurant or a fancy buffet. I have taken the time to visit and learn these "new" departments from people working at ground level. My job as a manager is to make the lives of the employees easier. I can only do that if I understand what it is they do and who they are. Having worked my way from the bottom, through the departments to my current position gives me a whole picture perspective (balcony view if you like that sort of thing). I see the whole picture, I don't see Casinos as an "Auditor" or "Manager" or "Floor Worker;" I see it from all the perspectives. The top positions need someone who can step out of any single view of the casino and see it in-total. Many in positions of upper management of the regimes have never seen a casino from the ground floor. They do not have the unique perspective that brings to the table. It not only informs your choices, but it builds trust amongst your staff. My suggestion to you is to learn that ground level. Meet the people who are the boots on the ground, get to know them.

"Servant-Leadership" is a big part of my management style. My employees know that I am someone they can talk to and bring their problems. I am willing to listen and help both professionally and personally. I serve them because that is what a manager is, a servant. The idea of servant leadership is important in a native casino because they are geared not just toward making a profit but also toward improving a community and enriching a tribe. The managers at another business can often ignore the employees' personal problems because they are only looking for productive employees. Managers in Indian Country must go deeper because our goal is not just for employees to be productive at work, but to be productive at home. Managers in Indian Country are in the position where we employ our sisters and brothers, our cousins and spouses. We don't want to work our employees into the ground and then get more. That employee is our friend, our family member. Servant Leadership is great in its ability to care not just for the bottom line, but also for the whole employee. It is my pride to turn each area I manage into a family. I am excited for the world we live in as more and more businesses take on this more holistic approach to management. Companies everywhere are learning to build up their employees through compassion and trust.

Though I am an enrolled member of the Village of Kotzebue and a shareholder of NANA Corp I grew up on the Coeur d'Alene Reservation. My family and ties are all interwoven with that Tribe and Tribal Community. Coming from Indian Country and having ties from it is important to me. When I think of how to better my family and my community I think of putting money into Tribes and

Tribal programs. I work hard to remain sensitive to the needs of a Tribal Community and Tribal Members because I grew up on the reservation. I was raised by Tribal Elders, and have many native relations that are enrolled Coeur d'Alene. When I see ex-drug addicts trying to work at the Casino and improve themselves, I do not help them because of some external wish to help people. I help them because I know them. They were seniors when I was a freshman. Their mom is a friend with my mom. Their dad helped teach me to hunt as a child. When I stop and talk to elders at the casino or in life it is because I know and care for them. I mowed their lawn as a kid. They probably swatted my butt or gave me candies as a child. They taught me lessons in life I needed to learn, and they will teach me more. I talk to them because like your children I was taught these people were to be respected and cared for. Not some strangers I should listen to, but individual people I should respect. I grew up on the reservation and I bring a sensitivity to the relationships that exists when you are part of a Tribal Community. Management positions within Indian Country need someone who can be sensitive to the needs and people who own and work for the Casino. Do not be an outsider deciding what is best for strangers. Be a friend asking, how you can help your family. If you want to live and work in Indian Country you really need to learn this lesson.

I know that many of the elders I speak to are proud of my going out and getting my degrees, and I am proud as well. But I am also very aware of who I owe. I am aware of the duties that engenders. The Coeur d'Alene Tribe has nurtured and raised me, its membership has shaped me and helped me become the man I am today. I in turn pay it back by committing to serving communities in the same way they taught me. I feel a deep duty to not only the Coeur d'Alene Tribe but Indian Country and Indian Gaming in particular. Not just as a member of its community, but also as a family member. I write my books to help engender a better understanding for those managers in and coming in to our industry. I also write to help grow the managers that are here already. Indian Gaming has done so much to shape and better my life and family. I now want to help shape and better it through service. The people of Indian Gaming have become part of my family. I am honored in keeping alive the vision, the ideals, and the success of that family through this book and books like it.

I have an AA, AS, BS, and an MBA. I am a semester away from my Law Degree. Legal training is extremely helpful in the gaming world. Top Gaming Managers are forced to deal with ever changing legal restrictions, and MICS compliance. They have to work hand in hand with the Tribe, State, and Federal governmental agencies to understand and interpret the law. A needed skill that only a legal degree can truly prepare one for. The workings of the gaming world are entrenched with legalese and attorneys. This is something Indian Gaming executives must understand for our continued success.

Legal training does not stop with the law. It also teaches one how to network, dig out information, and listen to our client's stated needs. It teaches one how to put our client's desires above our own. And most importantly, how to take complex and emotional situations and break them down into options for our

client. Sometimes the Casino will be faced with choices that only

the Tribe can make. The managers need to be able to set down

the problem efficiently and understandably with a good

explanation on each available option. They need to be capable of

explaining why he or she would choose a particular path. Legal

training prepares you to explain complex legal terms to those who

have not had a lifetime of learning them. It opens you to

accepting the client's ultimate choice, and finding a way to make

it work. My educational background has prepared me to do this.

For all the gatekeeping in the world it is a thing easily learned for

those of you reading this and committed to trying to learn. You

must dedicate yourself to be able to understand complex business

and legal concepts, and explain them to a layperson.

My first book "Becoming a Trust Based Supervisor" went

over some very basic supervisor training and things I have learned

over the years managing people. This book you are reading will

focus on the analytics and basics of the Casino Floor. I focus on mainly slot accounting, settings, placement, and casino layouts. Really just how the day to day building, maintaining, and growing a casino works. Finally my third book (yet to be written) will go over working in Indian Country. I will be focusing mainly on the laws and politics involved. These first three books are not big complex affairs, but simple books for those just starting out.

I had originally wanted to write a long winded in depth book on slot accounting and analysis to help teach others about how to understand the numbers and things I was doing within my own organization. As I thought about it more and looked at books on the market I realized that is not what most people need. They did not need what to them would be a long expensive compilation of every way analysis worked. And honestly if they did there are a few good ones out there. What they needed was a simplified breakdown of what all the words mean and a quick tutorial on how to use them. I am sure other slot directors and slot analysts understand my frustration in dealing with highly intelligent people who have little to no idea about what I am talking about. From

Tribal members wanting to understand what the casino is doing to executives in other areas. I find the words of Casino Operations are often confusing. This book is designed to be given to those people so that they have a baseline reference to what we are doing. Why we are doing it. And what the multitude of words mean. If you are a slot analysts this will be more of a reference and I am guessing only the first of many such books you will be reading in your career.

I hope you enjoy this book. Slot accounting is one of my favorite things in the world to do. It is filled with nuisances and leaps of understanding that few other number based statistics have. It is a science and an art form all rolled into one. It allows you to build and maintain a thing of beauty. A temple of gold.

Part 1

Slot Analysis a Quick Run Down

At the start of the book I am going to give a quick rundown of slot analysis. I will jump right into leased games then move through some basics of building a casino floor. I will then move on to a more in-depth reading of slot analysis. You should be doing this analysis weekly, monthly, quarterly, and annually. This is to ensure that your floor is in tip top shape. I do not advocate official/formal meetings where everybody goes over the documents. I suggest on your own you weekly go over. A basic look. Follow this up where monthly and quarterly you go over a much more in-depth look. And finally annually you go over a full year's worth of numbers. I then suggest you have several staff members who do the same that you can discuss the numbers with. They will run them different than you, and that can only add benefit to the analysis. If you go over them together in every part, you will find you all see the same thing. You want different eyes, for a broader view. Once you have a cadre of folks looking at numbers you have people within the organization you can talk to about how games or sections are doing. Almost daily someone informally asks if I noticed certain machines and how well (or lack thereof) they are doing. This allows your organization to have an organic constant dialogue about how things are going. I am a big believer in organic dialogue being a better communication system then strict formal meetings. That said they both should take work. If you find those you trust are not approaching you it is time to find new people.

I do suggest more formal meetings around each quarter, before purchases, and during/around changes. If you keep up on the informal discussions, this should be plenty. These meetings are more forced and less organic. If you are keeping up with your consistent dialogues they should start to come naturally. The analysis should be driving gaming floor decisions. Everyone who is part of that process should be running their own analysis. They should be taking part in the informal and formal discussions.

Here in this section I start with a quick and simple run down. I want for beginners to be able understand the terms I will use throughout the book. I attempted to cut back on the amount of terms. Many systems use different names, and I did try to cut that back in all of this for ease of learning. Remember the goal here is open the door for everyone hearing the numbers reported to be able to understand and participate in conversations. I want a marketing director to not fear sounding foolish when asking a question and a CEO that can grasp what they hear without playing 20 questions.

Chapter 1

Let's Jump Right In

If this first part seems confusing to you do not worry. It is meant to get a basic idea into your head so that as I move through all the other sections you already have a quick overview. The real lessons come later. This is just a quick, "so you know section." I imagine you will start off going back and forth between chapter 1 and chapter 2 as you get comfortable.

Let us jump right in (Please note the hold will not become important or even accurate until you start to have cash outs):

For example if someone puts $10 into a nickel machine, spins $5. Wins $4. And is now left with $9.00. The basic break down in analysis is that the machine's numbers looks like this:

Denom	0.05
Days	1
Coin in	5
Coin out	4
Cash drop	10
Ticket drop	0
Ticket Out	0
Jackpots,	0
Win	0
per unit	0
Hold %	20%

The player is left with $9 on the game. Now say they spin again for $5. This time hitting $10. The player now has $14 in credits.

Denom	0.05
Days	1
Coin in	10
Coin out	14
Cash drop	10
Ticket drop	0
Ticket Out	0
Jackpots,	0
Win	0
per unit	0
Hold %	-140%

Ok now the player is feeling pretty lucky. They spin $10.00 and receive only $2.00 in return. The game has left them with $6.00 in credits which they then cash out. The analysis now looks like this:

Denom	0.05
Days	1
Coin in	20
Coin out	16
Cash drop	10
Ticket drop	0
Ticket Out	6
Jackpots,	0
Win	4
per unit	4
Hold %	20%

The player decides to try again. They throw in their $6.00 ticket and another $10.00, and spin $5.00. They finally hit a jackpot for $1250.00. Now the player has a single win where they received more than $1200.00. Because of this the win must be handled by an attendant and a W2G filled with the IRS. The player also has $11.00 left in credits. They cash out. The analysis now finally looks like this:

Denom	0.05
Days	1
Coin in	25
Coin out	1266
Cash drop	20
Ticket drop	6
Ticket Out	17
Jackpots,	1250
Win	-1221
per unit	-1221
Hold %	-49%

Hopefully as a short example of the numbers this will help you to get comfortable before we move on.

Chapter 2

A Quick Cheat Sheet in Terms

Denom is the amount the machine's credit is worth. This game is a "nickel" game, means that the game understands all nickels as a base of one. All payouts are then multiplied by $.05, hence if the machine says that a line pay pays 400 credits, it would equate to $20.00. Most modern games can be toggled between credit amount and dollar amount. Thus making it easier to tell how much actual cash is left on the game. Most modern reporting systems use dollar amounts for their analysis. If you ever need to take hard meters straight from the game you will need to convert credits metered to actual cash amounts.

Days or DOF is the amount of days the machine was online during the analysis. Here we are only looking at a single day, and

the machine was online that day. This metric is necessary to

create apples to apples comparisons between machines.

Coin in is the amount the machine was spun. As you can

see every time the game was spun it increased the coin in. The

coin in is really an indicator of time on device (so volume). The

longer the gambler continues to spin, regardless of the amount

lost or won, this number grows. The industry currently debates if

Coin in or Net Win are the most important indicators of the value

of a game. Coin in shows the actually amount of time and energy

a player is willing to dedicate to a single machine regardless of

what the casino makes off said game. Net win, as you will see

below, is an indicator of money made or lost by the casino. I

would recommend you look at all the numbers. But these two are

really vital to ensure a quick understanding of a games value.

After looking at these you can more easily drill down into the

other areas to check the full picture.

Coin Out is the amount the machine paid over the entire experience. As you can see it does not equal the amount the customer takes home. It is just the amount the machine paid back during each spin even if that payback was less than the amount spun. Just like the coin in, this number only goes up.

Drop is the amount in the cash box. This box will contain tickets and cash. As you can see they are separated on the analysis. There is often two following numbers, "metered drop" and "actual drop" on most sheets. For simplicity I did not add them here. Metered drop is what the machine thinks is in the box. Actual drop is what is actually counted by the drop and count team. As you can imagine the goal is to ensure these numbers match. To many variances can indicated something wrong with your count process.

This number can be exaggerated if a player puts in a lot of cash but only plays a small amount and cashes out. Likewise if they put in large amounts of tickets, cash out every few spins, and then reenters the tickets. Really any other crazy formula customers can come up with to increase their luck can effect this in odd ways. A skewed drop can also indicate money laundering and is worth investigating.

Ticket Out, is the amount of all tickets the machine has generated through player cash outs. This is money the player actually takes from the machine. Again players can increase this by cashing out a lot then reentering that ticket only to cash out again.

Jackpots, handpays, and cancel credits are the combined amount of all attendant pays. If an attendant must come to the machine and give the customer cash for any reason it is referred to as a handpay and it is entered in this area. It is also often referred to as "actual attendant payouts." It is usually jackpots and machine malfunctions.

Two common additions next to Jackpots in separate lines are "fills" and "bonus." As modern machines make fills obsolete and most modern bonus now are handled through the standard

play or as a jackpot these two sections are really more and more

useless and unused in analysis. For reference, I have never seen a

fill at a modern casino (though you will if you use hard coin), and I

have seen bonus used to track an early lucky coin jackpot, but

that was years and years ago. The fill is the amount of coin an

attendant "fills" the game with.

Net Win is the end of day metric casinos' use. It indicates

the amount of money they actually made off of that machine.

The Net Win is created from a simple mathematical formula based

off of hard meters from the machine. That formula is: *(Actual*

Cash Drop + Actual Ticket Drop) – (Ticket out + Jackpots + Bonus

+Fills) = Net Win. You can then divide the total Net Win by days

in service to get at the "per unit" number. In a similar way we

often divide the coin in by the days in service in order to get a

daily coin in. Creating daily numbers is a way of allowing for

easier comparison amongst machines. Basically take everything

that went into the machine, and subtract everything that came out of it, and you get what you made off the game.

The **hold** percentage here is equated out by dividing the win by the coin in. When setting up a machine the techs will put in a "par %" which has an inverse relationship with the hold %. Meaning that if the machine is set at 90% Par, then the hold should equate out to 10%. The hold is an indicator of the percentage of every dollar spun that the casino should keep from each machine. So the player wants this number as low as possible. A machine with a hold % of 10% should be keeping roughly $.10 of every dollar spun in the machine over a set period of time. The higher a number the hold % is then the "tighter" or "colder" the machine is. And the less money the customer is likely to win (the par obviously is opposite). There are several methods to calculate the hold, but this is the most common and widely used for slot accounting.

It is an important note here that there are a variety of methods of calculating the hold. Table games for example use a different system. You must be sure that the hold you are comparing uses the same calculation you used.

Serial Numbers: are the number that comes with the machine from the manufacturer and stay with the game forever. It is purely a labeling and tracking device.

Asset numbers: are the numbers assigned based on denom, and change only when the denom, theme, or other set conversions take place. Moving a machine will not change an asset number. It is also a labeling and tracking device.

Location Number: This number represents where a machine sets on the floor. It changes when the machine is moved, but not when it is converted, etc. Between the asset and location numbers things will often cause one to change but not the other. It is again a labeling and tracking device.

Machine Number: This phrase is used often interchangeably with either the asset number or the location number. I use it for the location number. I just as often see it used for the asset. In an attempt to avoid confusion I will just not

use it. If I slip up and you see it in the book, know that for me it is

almost always the location number.

Chapter 3

How Do We Use It

When first looking at a series of machines to determine how they are doing you first look at coin in. Usually daily coin in. This number is a good indicator of popularity as it is a pure volume indicator. The more a game gets played the higher this number goes. We like games to have a high coin in, as it shows that customers are willing to put time on device.

Once you sort by coin in you can start looking at Win per Unit. This number tells you what the casino actually made off a machine. You have to do math for participation and leased games so you can see what you win after fees. Remember this can have a dramatic effect, especially in the case of WAPs where the lease is based on coin in. I have targeted companies that will give us

Caps (a dollar amount you do not pay over (often $50.00)),

though there is still one and only one company with a minimum, a

dollar amount you never pay bellow ($20- $35). Because of their

refusal to budge this manufacturer will be removed completely

soon off my floor.

We have to take a tangent at this point to see any

discrepancies in these two numbers. They should both

theoretically rise and fall together. This is not always the case. If

the hold % is skewed the coin in will grow slower than the win or

vice versa. The most common thing you will see in disconnect is a

high Coin in and a low to negative Win. The reason this happens

is usually jackpots. If a machine hits a large jackpot, it's win and

hold percentages will skew badly for days to months. This

disconnect is an important tangent to take at this point to ensure

you are correctly valuing the game. The game may for a short

time have a low to negative win, but still be valuable. Just be sure

that you red flag it to keep an eye on it.

After you have looked at these two numbers to determine a games value, you can start to break apart why the numbers are as they are. The main variables in different values for the same theme, are location, settings, denom, you have too many of that theme, and if the game was down. You will compare same machine with other machines in the casino that are different based on these criteria and anything else unique to a specific game.

Location can have a big impact, especially non-smoking (down), C-stores, and bars. If a game is smoking hot everywhere but one area, moving it can increase its numbers. If it is doing good "for its location" we might leave it there to ensure variety in all the areas. You will have to learn your hot and cold spots for your casino. Cold spots where you do not really care about the machine mix in that area are a good place for legacy (read old) games with a strong following. Customers will search them out even in the worst areas.

Denom is something you need to find the correct setting

for as different games do better or worse in different denoms. As example when we tried Cashlines as a dollar instead of pennies their numbers dramatically increased to top performers. Do not rely on what the manufacturer designed the theme to be. I found G+ games designed for lower denom do great as a dollar and five dollar game.

Settings are important, and it is a thing you look at mostly with multi-game/multi options like video poker and keno. They have multiple versions of software and the settings to be chosen. Discovering which setting the majority of customers want or prefer is vital. These setting can be lines, reels, options, multigame choices, odds, etc. Do not be afraid of trial and error. I have often built a few different banks with differing options and then listened to the customers and watch the numbers.

We have too many, can result in low numbers across the board. Or low numbers in just a few set games. If they are all banked together, the exterior games will often outperform the interior. The larger the bank the more the interior drops. Cutting down the size of the bank, or limiting the number of themes may even this out. It is also the most likely time when you will receive complaints for removing games, as the game you remove is always someone's favorite. Every game is someone's favorite.

If the **machine is down**, obviously its numbers will drop. Knowing the history and value of the games that are down allows your techs to target the higher value games to fix first. Why spend 8 hours and $1000 to fix a $50.00 a day game when you could get that $500.00 a day game up in a few hours. Prioritization is a key reason for analysis.

Once you know how a game is doing you can determine what to do with it. Any changes you make you should agree to give a set time as a test. 30-90 days is standard. I usually play it partially by ear. And to be honest with major or impactful changes I am usually looking at the numbers pretty soon after the fact. This honestly as comforting as it is, isn't very helpful, as the numbers skew the shorter the time frame you look at. And customers take time to learn the change.

It is important to remember when there are issues that will skew your numbers so you can mentally adjust your valuation of the games in question. I always pretend I am going to have to explain to someone why the numbers are crazy. I then work out how I would explain it. I find this mental exercise helps me to better understand the numbers. It also has the side benefit that it helps when someone really does ask about the numbers. If you are unable to internally explain it to yourself that is a pretty big indicator that the game deserves a closer look.

Part 2

Leased and Participation Games

You will not always wish to purchase every game. That said you will need to keep your floor updated. A way to do this is through leased and participation games. The most common leased games are Wide Area Progressives (WAPs). WAPs are not only usually big impressive games, but have a jackpot base amount of $100,000 to $1 million dollars. Seeing as most casinos cannot afford to pay out a million dollar jackpot on their own, Leased games are a good alternative. Leased games are paid based off a percentage of coin in.

This is different than participation games which are paid based off a flat fee or a percentage of the win. Participation games do not have the big jackpots, but often contain bonuses or features otherwise unavailable for purchase. Participation is also a good way to test new games you are thinking of purchasing but are unsure of their real value. You can also demand the manufacturer maintains a tech presence to keep the games working and maintained. This helps in cutting back on tech costs. If you have a good tech department this is not actually as big of a savings as you might imagine. I have been blessed with some amazing internal techs in my life so the benefit of manufacturer techs is back and forth. I have found that I have always preferred my own in-house techs once I have put in the effort to get them trained and hire for skill.

For your floor the mix of leased and participation in regards to your overall floor percentage is something your casino will need to decide. I suggest no more than 20% and no less than 5%. I prefer to see a floor to set about 10-11% to keep a good mix of new high end games flowing through for your customers without paying manufacturers the bulk of your profits. I will discuss both forms of manufacturer owned games and then some

ideas on how to ensure that you fully understand the worth of the

games you have and help you ensure you are getting the most out

of them.

Daniel Hansen

Chapter 4

Leased Games

Leased games are manufacturer owned games that usually sell as a large jackpot that is linked across many casinos. If the jackpot is hit the manufacturer pays it out. The fees for such games are usually based on the games coin in with 3.2%-4.5% being the average fee that you will find. Always look for the lowest percentage.

The better the game, the bigger the jackpot, the higher the fee. Traditional forms of this game are Wheel of Fortune, Mega Bucks, or Wizard of Oz. Many players will seek out casinos that have these games in order to ensure they can have a life changing jackpot. Casino's offer these games to offer their customers' life changing jackpots without the casino itself being responsible for paying it out.

Though a million dollar jackpot can have a strong pull for customers, these games have their drawbacks. First, the manufacturer is often much stricter with options the game may have. Second, they often have the tightest hold percentage of any game on a casino floor. The casino has no real control over what that hold may be. Lastly, the casino will also usually not have any real control over the other settings of the game. They are often forced to accept whatever the manufacturer offers for that particular theme and jackpot.

Leased games also usually have a much higher bill at the end of the month then a standard participation game. Without the option of flat rates, and fees being based off of coin in it adds up. A well-played leased game will often pull 30%-45% of the games win. Meaning that even if the game is loved by customers and brings in a large customer base the casino will not make as much off a leased game as they will off other participation games. And much less then off of games they own.

It is paramount that when choosing leased games you pick

games that will attract customers that otherwise may not have

chosen your casino, or that you choose leased games that

gamblers expect to see on your floor. Of the 10% I suggest for

manufacturer owned games, I would suggest no more than 2%-4%

be leased. This is to ensure the casino is not paying out its profits

to the manufacturer. I would also suggest that you wait to

negotiate leased games at the same time you are negotiating a

purchase. Doing this you can use an increase in these valuable

commodities to help negotiate a better price on conversions and

game purchases. There is no reason that you should not be able

to utilize a little strong arm tactics with manufacturers to lower

other prices for them to gain valuable floor space.

Chapter 5

Participation

Participation games do not have the big jackpots that leased games have. That said they often come with sign packages, special bonus and preferably some sort of local area progressive (LAP) which will only progress based on play from your casino. Participation games are a good way to ensure that you have signs and new pretty games rotating throughout your floor without the capital expense of game purchases. They are also a good way to try standard games you are thinking of purchasing but are unsure how they will do, especially new manufacturers. When negotiating these games, especially with new manufacturers, it is good to request free trials. Include a built in option to purchase the game (most commonly with at

33

least 90 days of fees going toward the purchase costs). I cannot stress enough negotiate first. That way if the game does amazing you are not pressured to pay more than you wanted to pay. It will be harder to talk down a salesperson when they see the 8 times house average numbers the game may do. And let's face it if the game does poorly you will not even ask to buy it.

Once you are negotiating these games it is good to know the options for fees. Flat fees are good for games that you know are going to do well. Mega Meltdown is a good example of a game you are going to want in small doses with a flat fee (if possible). It usually does well over house average and if you are stuck with a percentage of win, the percentage will most likely be well over any flat rate you can negotiate. Flat rates can range from $15-$60 a day. With the better games demanding a higher rate than games past their prime or ones that are untested.

Several manufacture also will offer special add-ons to games you own for a small daily fee. Game King is famous for this with the many add-on games you can get. The use of these add-ons should be looked into, They should also closely watched.

Why pay a manufacturer a portion of your profits if their special

bonus does not increase your win.

The standard participation fee in the industry has been

80/20 for several years. Some manufacturers have been toying

with 85/15 and 80/20 with a license fee. The most common

though will be an 80/20 split. This means the casino is taking 80%

of the win.

You will want to ensure to never accept a manufacturer

that has minimum fees as this will cut into your overall profits if

they are not keeping up on their games. It also indicates they do

not have faith in their own product.

For example if a manufacturer has a $35.00 flat fee and

the game drops to $100 a day win, you are faced with paying out

$35 instead of $20. This is 35% of the win instead of the 80/20

split that is the industry average. I cannot stress enough

minimums are usually only added if the manufacturer has no faith in their own product making money on your floor. Honestly if they don't have faith in their own game, why would you even add it?

On the flip side are caps or maximums. Always request caps. No matter how many times you are told no (and you will hear no) you ask for them. Caps are the opposite of minimums, in that they are maximums. This means you tell the manufacturer, you will pay 80/20 or a cap (say $50) whichever is less. In the modern world of the industry, caps are becoming more and more common amongst manufacturers that have a strong faith in their product and also offer flat fees.

They do this because they have faith in their product to outperform the cap, ensuring that their 80/20 is really just a flat fee. I have had little problem with manufacturers like Konami or Aruze accepting this. Their product is almost always going to be in the top performers, and they will always hit the cap, every month. I have had Konami participation on my floor now 10 years and even the oldest one I have never paid less than the cap.

Chapter 6

Adjusting Your Slot Analysis

Your slot analysis will need to be adjusted for any manufacturer owned games. You do this rather simply by adding a few extra lines in your excel sheet. Ok here we get technical and computery. First add a column where you can enter the fee agreement, such as 20% or 4.2%, then add a second column where you tell excel to do the math (i.e. (=flat fee), (win*(participation/100)) or (coin in*(lease/100))) this will give you the amount you are paying the manufacturer. Remember to add in any minimums or maximums with true or false functions in excel. Now that you know the amount you are paying the manufacturer you will want to add a third column where you subtract the fee amount from the machine's win. This will give you the amount you actually made off that particular game.

222

I usually at this point also add a fourth column to see what percentage of the win I am paying to the manufacturer. Or vice versa, the percentage I am actually keeping (all your preference). I have found that showing a casino the percentage they are paying on their leased games especially is often eye opening to why you want to limit these games to small elite sections of your floor.

So now you know the dollar amount you are really making off of your leased games. How do you use it? It is important to remember that you are giving a portion of your profits to the manufacturer for the right to have these games on you floor. It is only your due diligence to ensure the casino is benefiting from such a tradeoff. The common question to ask yourself is, do I have customers coming in my door just for these games, or are they staying longer to play them, because if I do not, those customers would have come in my door and spent the same money in games I own. That is a long sentence but you should read it again and understand it. If my answer is not yes it indicates, I am just throwing money away. You can poll your customers. You can listen to those customers that demand or request specific games. But that only gives the answer for those customers who speak up. The most straightforward method is ensure that your leased games after all fees are doing at least twice house average in win. If a participation game cannot do at least twice house, it is just not a strong enough pull for you to keep on your floor. It is good to watch the coin in as well, but it be funds the casino nothing for players to push higher coin in on these games without you making any money off them. I also suggest having your rewards points harder to obtain on the leased games. Things like free play be turned off so as not to build unmerited coin in on games.

At the end of the day your job is to ensure your customers have fun games to play so that the casino makes more money. Lease and participation can help ensure a steady stream of updated games. Still you must ensure you limit the cost to the casino as much as possible to ensure that you are not over spending on something that only adds minimal benefit. Please make sure you keep a close eye on these games. Stay on your

sales rep to ensure they are changing out your games as

frequently as needed to keep the games relevant. The end all be

all keep your floor active.

Part 3

Game Purchases

It is important to keep your floor as refreshed as possible. There will be those old games that players just love that you keep running long past their lifespan, for no other reason than their long legs that just keep on running. Those games that need to be on your floor for it to feel like a casino to patrons. But for the most part to ensure your casino stays relevant and your customers happy, you must purchase new games and conversions.

Conversions are a way to change a theme without buying a brand new box. If conversions, location changes, and game setting changes just will not up the game's value it is time to start

looking at purchases for replacement. Purchases will range from

different cabinets and vendors to ensure your floor keeps a solid

flow, good sight lines, and a wide range of options for players to

choose from. One of the goals of slot analysis is to ensure the

games on your floor are still relevant. Just because a game is

smoking hot today, does not mean next month anyone will care to

play it. Do not become trapped by past numbers.

Chapter 7

Options to try Before Purchase

The first option I would suggest if a game is starting to fail is a location change. Every casino has hot spots and cold spots. Locations that just rock and roll, and locations that just kill a theme. Non-smoking, cubby holes, poor lighting, and poor ventilation can all attribute to a locations poor performance. By moving a low performer into a better location you can test if it is just the game that sucks or the location. Another method of checking this is if you have multiple games with the same theme. Check the performance of all these game themes in different locations. This will help you determine the games value without even having to move it. If the theme sucks in non-smoking, but is rocking outside the bar, it might be beneficial to move that theme over by the bar. Location is a litmus test. Bad locations may need

rethought, and revamped, rather than revamping the games

within it. If there is nothing you can do, throw legacy games here.

They have a following or they would not still be around at that

age.

Quick note, a beginner's mistake is to look at your analysis

and see that you have 30 games of the same theme and think

they all suck. Think that you need to dump them all. My

suggestion is to drop the amount of games you have of this

theme. You might just be over saturated. By cutting back on how

many you have, the remaining few should increase in revenue.

The second option is game settings. I have often seen crappy

penny games do a complete turnaround when made a dollar. And

poor performing dollar games sky rocket when made into

pennies. Other settings are max bet, line options, hold

percentage, and any other option the particular theme has that

you can change. To you the changes may be small. To the player

it may make or break their gaming experience. Be sure to

communicate any setting changes to floor staff as customers are used to playing the game one way. They will be asking what happened to "their game." The last thing you want the floor staff to say, is, "what? Are you sur it is not the same." They should use this as an upsell. A way to tell the customer that the casino is trying to improve their gaming experience. A setting change that depends on your backend system or ability to offer it, is to add a jackpot to your lowest performing bank. Advertise it with casino signage and through floor staff. This will often be a true test. A game with a loose jackpot that cannot attract customers is a game no longer worth having.

The third option may cost you some money. That is conversions. First, ask for free conversions from those manufacturers you have participation with. Your sales rep should be motivated to keep you happy, and it is often good to at least ask. It you might save a few bucks. Purchase prices of conversions can range from $800-$4000 depending on manufacturer and quality of the game. The average starting price being about $2000-3000. A conversion package can really turn a game around. With a new theme, new glass, new options. An old and dying cabinet can have new life breathed into it. Your players will often assume you actually bought new games. This of course depends on the quality of the conversion. A good method to ensure this perception is to move the cabinet at the same time you convert the game. Some manufacturers just have nothing worth replacing their old themes with, and then it is time buy a new game from a different vender.

Chapter 8

Let's Purchase Some Games

So you need to purchase some games. First thing you want to do is look at competitors and other casinos. See what vendors are doing well. What cabinets are technologically sound. It does nothing for your customers to have new and amazing games they either do not want to play or games that are never up and running.

It is important that you garner a good network of other casino executives that you can call and ask these kinds of questions. In return make yourself available to assist in their questions. Networking ensures that when your sales rep says, "we have never seen/done that." You know they are being honest or hedging. Trust me even the nice ones lie.

After doing your due diligence on what your customers will want in terms of game type and game style start calling the vendors that are doing well elsewhere, or have the options you want.

Options to take into consideration are do you need high denom games, slant tops for sight lines, uprights for view blocking, progressive jackpots to attract attention, free spins, extensive bonuses, theme styles your customers like (Egyptian, gods, dolphins, Asian, native, etc.). Remember these are not the stuff you may like, but what your customers want. What your floor needs. Once you know what you want, how many, and what you have to spend you are ready. So start trolling the sales reps.

A note here I know the sales reps are your friends. You have probably went to dinner with them. Maybe a few drinks. Crack a few jokes. Share a few friendships and funny stories. But at the end of the day your job is to get a good deal for the casino.

Their job is to increase their company's margins. Do not forget

that. Anything you can use to ensure you get a good price, you

use. Win-win is always best, but you make your deal not theirs.

There will be no shortage of sales reps wanting a piece of

your capital budget. Make sure they all know you are looking, and

that you are talking to all of them. If possible, this is a good time

to negotiate participation and leased games. By tying in an extra

bank or two of participation you get a better deal on purchase.

Also do not be afraid to let them know what other manufacturers

are offering. I never tell them who the other manufacturer is. But

you would be surprised at how far a simple, "everyone else is

offering me 10 new games for a 30% discount" can go. Or even, "I

have another manufacturer who does better on my floor that is

only charging $14,000."

I try not to ever lie, but I do wave the flag of the best deal

to the other sales reps. They want the deal. They will find a way.

They may not be able to match it, but they will become more

motivated to make a deal. Also make sure they know how many

games you are looking to buy, and what their piece of that pie "might be." Expect them to try and increase their share, and use that motivation to ensure a decent price. I never want to waste their time, but I likewise do not want my time wasted.

There is no reason to be a jackass, but there is also no reason to be a pushover. Make sure you throw in anything you might want, and see what they come back with. Have 50 games not doing well, and 20 of them are their games. Maybe offer them a purchase of 10 games if they throw in 10 conversions for 20 of those games.

An interesting technique I once witnessed but have never tried was a casino that had the slot manager begin negotiations. Once they had made some kind of deal with the sales rep, the slot manager said, "oh now I have to get approved by the Slot Director." The slot manager encouraged the sales rep to make a deal cause, "man we want those games." And the Slot Director did their best to drive the best bargain they could with the sales rep. They pushed for all the goodies and the best that they could offer. Once that contract was created, the Slot Director would call

the sales rep and say something like, "man we really want these

games. I just love the deal we made, but man my GM is just being

unreasonable. Is there anything I can offer her to make her feel

like we are getting something special."

I am not saying to try this tactic, but I can say the casino I

know that uses it swears by it. The Slot Manager gets to be the

good guy, even the Director continues a good relationship with

the sales rep, but the three step negotiation gets them better and

better deals. At the end of the day you need to find your own

techniques that will fit with your property and the people who will

be part of the process.

As I said earlier I prefer the, "the other guy is beating that

deal." But it is important you find a negotiation method that fits

you and your organization. If you try and do something that just

doesn't fit who you are it will not be authentic. You will not do as

good a job ensuring your casino gets the best deal. I have made

some great friendships with salespeople. I have a high level of respect for the job they do. It is a balancing act to ensure that

everyone wins, no bridges are burnt, and you get the casino a

good deal. Happy negotiating.

Chapter 9

Placing Games

For a book built for novices and non-slot directors why do we need a section on placing games? What I am really trying to get across here for those that are not part of the placement is a shallow end look at how it happens. Too often people not in the position to place games just assume placement and settings are done randomly or in a desire to build a maze like affect. But trust me if those creating your floor layout are doing their jobs then there is a lot of forethought going into the positions. We are looking for a certain feel while combing the current data on what players want and what will increase their time on device. It looks like chaos but there is science and art to the process they are using. So let's jump in.

53

Now that you have bought some new pretty games, how do you determine where to place them? Well first what is the cabinet style? Slant tops are usually used for sight lines and allowing players to see other games or amenities past them. This puts pretty games in the front of the casino, but still allows players to see all the glory of your floor in the background. Slants have the added benefit of not requiring bases, which can be a nice bonus in cost. (On a side note: Most modern manufacturers are slowing ruining sightlines by making slants taller and taller, and reducing their benefit for sight lines.) But the older slants should be placed in areas where you want customers to come to an area and be able to see great things in the distance. See the fun games right in front of them and also a bank or two away. It creates the impact of overload. There are flashing lights here, and there, and look at all of that. It gives them a moment's pause to enjoy the art you are trying to create with your floor. Too many floor layouts forgo this understanding that a slot floor is art. It should be a thing of beauty that can be first appreciated, and then dived into and experienced.

Does the game have a sign package? If so against a far wall, or in the midst of other games away from entrances and walkways are a good spot to look for. By putting these signs a little off the beaten path it gives your customers a reason to explore. Gamblers often want to wander. They want to find 'that game,' 'their game.' That is the game they came to play. And by giving them a destination they can see and seek out, they will walk past a multitude of other games they may wish to try and experience.

It changes their visit from a come in sit down and dump money into the same game over and over, into a true gambling adventure. By building your floor from slants to signs, mixing low and high games to ensure sight lines, and areas that open up, and other areas that close in, you ensure the players have a real experience. A chance to look around and be surprised when they turn a corner. Feel safe and alone when they find that cozy spot. Mapping the floor with something like AutoCAD is the first step.

But you really must walk it once the games are in place. Stand in different areas, and see what your customers will see. Modify the floor as often as needed. It should be organic. It should grow and change, and mold to the customers' changing needs.

Is it high denom? If so place it where your high rollers want to play it. You must learn these areas. Do you have a high denom area? Is that where they will want it? Do they like alley ways, or do they prefer hidden coves where only other high rollers see them? Each group is different. I would suggest getting to know your players of this caliber. That way you can ensure their happiness.

I would even suggest that after you place the games, you offer a way for the big players to try them for free. Then you ask them, would they like them somewhere else, different settings, etc.? Making these players happy is paramount.

If you have a high denom area, it is hopefully the only area you have mixed cabinets in banks (note cabinet not theme.

Themes should be mixed across most of the floor). This is because you want your high denom players to have a broad selection, but they really do not need 10 banks of 6 games of each type. Oddly enough the high denom games will look dead most of the time. Trust in that Net Win, if it is high, they are playing them.

Are they legacy games that your players like? Games that have stood the test time. Games that have a following. Games that customers are coming in just to play. These games group in locations you know are not your triple A locations. For one, these games are often not as beautiful as the new games. Second, they will pull players into these areas. The players will follow the games. They have played them for 8 years, and they are not going to let the fact that they are in a non-prime location stop them from continuing to play them. Lastly, these locations mean you won't have to move this style of game as much. These players often want to just come to the casino. Find their specific game, and play it. They are not the explorers, or the appreciator of beauty that your other players are. They just want their game.

Give it to them and leave it where it is. If you do find the need to move these games, be sure to let your frontline staff know where they have gone. That way the players can get to them quickly and with minimal frustration.

Legacy games can also be bunched together. It is a modern method of bank creation to ensure that there is a good mix of like but different themes on each bank. Look for same cabinet, similar play, but different themes all on one bank. Keep the bank small. Maybe six games, eight tops. That is the modern banking strategy, but for legacy games it is different. Put up a 10 pack with each side being five exact same games. This gives these players easy access to what they want. It is important to offer each style of player something different. Something they want.

The legacy players want the old corn rows that most modern casinos and players scoff at. So find them an out of the way place and give it to them. I have found that seeding these style of banks in several different areas that need a boost and leaving them alone is the best. The players can easily find their legacy game. It actually helps frame other areas laid out in a more modern banking strategy of offset, differently shaped banks containing few machines. That said the bulk of your floor layout should be in the modern strategy. Keep banks small to midsized. Rotate themes, and throw in a circle or triangle here and there. Try for endcaps. Endcaps are prettier than the ugly side of a machine. And please at all cost avoid banks with mixed cabinet styles in all areas except against walls and high denom. Just a few walls, and in high denom areas.

Well now you have an idea on how you bought your games and placed them. Let's look at how you know how they are doing.

Part 4

Slot Analysis the Support Labels

I have added a practice slot analysis onto google drive so that you can download and practice with play numbers. I used the example of a small casino of about 300 games. I created it with only a background of 19 days. Because of this it makes sense for the numbers to be varied and unpredictable. Pretend for the sake of learning that you have just started at a new casino. This is the report they give you to determine what changes you should make at the casino. Or you could pretend to be a Tribal Member handed the analysis by casino management to inform you of what the casino has been doing.

Questions to ask yourself: What more information do you

need? What manufacturers or denoms are working and which are not? What sections may need looked at? What kind of banking strategy would you suggest they change? Look at how I broke down each grouping. Pick a few banks and pretend they are participation. Figure out what you would be paying with different fee structures based on what I have said about leased and participation games. Feel free to comment on the document. Download it and mess around to ensure you are comfortable with the numbers we are working with.

Here is the link:

https://drive.google.com/file/d/0B3H9gU1jTfZKSkNJWElF U0dJc1E/view?usp=sharing

It is good to remember that much of what you will be doing in slot analysis is statistics. I highly recommend both a statistics class/book and that you work to learn excel or other spreadsheets if slot analysis will become a major component of your career. With the modern world of pivot tables and quick formulas, you can save yourself hours of labor by having the computer do much of the work for you. Knowing how to navigate spreadsheets is only going to become more important as time goes on.

A good example of how statistics can help you best understand your slot analysis is the understanding between the mean and the median in averages. The mean is the average you will use most often. It is simply adding together every number and dividing by the amount of the numbers. So the mean of 30, 30, 50, 74, and 300 would be 96.8. The median of these numbers is the middle number when placed in sequential order (or if an odd number, the mean of the two center numbers). The median of these numbers would be 50. The average of the games on your floor is commonly referred to as your house average.

As I said the mean will be your most common method of averaging. That said often when you have radically diverging numbers the median can be extremely helpful. I often use a mixing of the two when I am dealing with a section that may contain a machine that recently hit a huge jackpot, or a few themes that do seven times the rest of the section. Rather than do a full median or full mean, I simply use the median method to remove an equal amount of top and bottom performers. Sometimes as few as one or two games. The idea is to just get rid of those games that will skew your overall results unfairly. Then do a mean calculation on the middle group. This way I get a truer picture of what my casino average really is.

I always first do a full mean calculation and compare and contrast the other calculations I do to it. Call me old fashion, but that true mean is just nice to know. But do not allow a machine that recently hit for $150,000 to sink an entire floor. Do not allow a single bank of two games doing 10 times house average to unfairly inflate your analysis. Your goal as you move forward in figuring out your averages is to be able to compare and contrast games fairly and accurately to tell if they are doing well or not.

Your goal then is to find the true value of the game in

comparison to the rest of your floor. You need to learn your specific floor. How it ebbs and flows. How the numbers should be adjusted and analyzed. If I come in and ask you about a game, you should be able to tell me how it is doing in comparison to house, location, denom, manufacturer, and any other variables you may face for your property.

My second piece of advice is know your floor, your customers, and your staff. Keep discussions open about games your players like. What games your floor staff see being played and by whom. You will be shocked at how well your frontline staff know your games, and which games are popular. Knowing your floor and the people on it is paramount to doing your due diligence for fully understanding the numbers. A gaming executive that refuses to walk their floor is simply not doing the job. Walk the floor. Look at the numbers and walk the floor again. Look on the floor for machines that jumped out in the analysis. Look in the analysis for games that jumped out to you on the floor.

So now let's dig in further to what these slot analysis words really mean and how we can start to judge value based on them. This part will concentrate on the terms that are mainly used as labels and support numbers, or numbers that can have a quick explanation. I want to ensure that we have a good understanding of what these labels mean before we dig into value analysis labels of the games. This part will contain areas that will change how you determine the criteria for a good or bad value in the next part. It is important to understand these labels and how they can affect your analysis before moving into the valuation.

A quick note the term "machine number" can be used in reference to several different numbers on the game though most casinos use it for either the asset number or the location number. I myself usually use it for the location number. Not defining how it is used can lead to confusion. In the hopes of removing that confusion I will use asset and location and attempt to avoid "machine number."

The areas of interest we will be going over are those

numbers and information that are commonly found on every

basic report. These headings are: Serial Number, Asset Number,

Location Number, Denom, MFR, Type, Description, Status, DOF,

Daily Coin, Metered Coin In, Coin Out, Metered Bill Drop, Metered

Coin Drop, Metered Voucher Drop, Metered Total Drop, Total

Drop Variance, Non-Deduct Bonus, Metered Adjusted Total Drop,

Actual Fills, Actual Attendant Payouts, Vouchers Issued, Win,

Average Win per Unit per Day, and of course Hold Percentage.

My goal in the first section is that when you look at a

report you understand what each heading means. Then in the

second part will be the slot analysis on what I am calling the value

analysis, i.e. figuring out what the actual value of each game

means.

Chapter 10

Serial Number, Type, Status, Non-Deduct Bonus, Actual Fill,

and DOF

First let me describe the titles you will most often skim

over in the modern gaming field. It is important to know what

these numbers mean and how to use them. They will rarely be

more than a quick check at the start of your slot analysis. A

simple explanation of what they mean is all we require here.

First is the Serial Number. This is the number that the

manufacturer gives the machine. The number is important as it is

the only number that will never change. It is assigned. You can

always find the game through the system and the files through

the serial number. It should be used for audit tracking. Beyond

that daily slot analysis barely touches it unless selling, buying, or

tracking a game that has went through multiple changes in the time period you are looking at. It is one of those elements that you only rarely really use, but when you do, it is vital.

Type of game, is misleading as it is simply the style of cabinet, i.e. video, stepper. As the lines between video and stepper are blurred this area is often no longer used. If available in your system use this for more useful info, such as multi-game or actual cabinet style. I would suggest you find a useful way to use it. Otherwise you will find yourself deleting this line to clean up your reports more often than not.

Status of the game is simply if the game is active or inactive. Some systems will tell you if the game is retired, sold, or warehoused on top of the two basic options. Really what you want to know from your basic slot analysis is if the machine is active. Active means that the game is online and playable. Active games are the ones you will most likely be running numbers on. Though if you are trying to remember what games you retired and how they did in comparison to the ones you kept you could look at the inactive machine list. A thing to remember is that you will be looking at the machines active during your analysis. Meaning if you do 30 days 3 months ago, you will be looking at games active during that time period.   Not the games that are necessarily active now.

Non-Deduct Bonus, is an area left in the spreadsheet for bonuses on games that are not reflected elsewhere in the numbers. When I first saw lucky coin and other system generated bonuses this is where I found them. As the systems became more advanced though, these bonuses were more and more reflected in attendant pays or somehow attributed on the game itself. I usually do a quick scan over the analysis to see if there are any non-deduct bonuses in the column and if so why they are there.

Actual Fills are for games with coin. In the olden days before TITO a machine paid players through coin that fell into the tray. These coins were not always enough to pay each win, or the machine would simply run out. An attendant then would have to take a bag of coins and refill the hopper. Assuming your casino is not so old that your games pay in this way you can mostly ignore this column. But it is good to know, as some casinos keep old style games as a throwback and to give that gaming experience players remember from days of old. It is also good to remember that much of the design of modern slot games owes its place to these old style coin based slot games. You would be surprised to learn how much of the technological marvels we call slot machines owe their design and features to the old crank games.

DOF or Days on the Floor is pretty much what it sounds like; how many days the game was on the floor. Now this number usually means the days the game was active on the floor. Meaning the game could have been placed and not turned on for a few days, and those days will not count into this total. It will only count those days the game was online. You may have to manually change this number for games that are down due to repair if your system does not track this correctly. Frequent conversations with your tech department will ensure you know which games will and will not be affected.   The importance of ensuring the DOF is accurate is so that when you create daily numbers such as Daily Coin or Per Unit, you will be dividing by the

correct number. A game that has a DOF of a 100 should have a

higher sum than a game that has been on the floor for 30 days. It

is important to know which number you should be dividing by to

ensure you are making an apples to apples comparison. I do not

know how many times I wondered why a machine's numbers

were so low only to realize it had been off during a weekend end

for repairs, which killed its averages. Once you start creating your

own formulas for Daily averages this number will become more

and more important.

Daniel Hansen

Chapter 11

Asset Number and Denom

The gaming machine's asset number is assigned the game when it is first entered into the system. It only changes when the game is in some way converted. This conversion can be a theme change or a denom change. The first number of most asset numbers will actually tell you the games denom (1 = $.01, 2 = $.02 3 = $.05, 4 = $.10, 5 = $.25, 6 = $.50, 7 = $1.00, 8 = $5.00). It is common for the asset number to be the main number you use in your slot analysis to label the game. It is the label that only changes when the game is changed in such a way as to affect your slot analysis. Moving the machine does not change the asset number, though as you will see later it will change the location number.

The denom value in most systems should equal the games credit value, but it may equal the games meter value. By this say you have a $.20 credit value for a game, every credit is worth $.20. The game settings are able to handle this but the system settings do not have the option. You would set the meter value with the system to a denom value that is divisible to the credit value (usually the largest number divisible). So in this example you could set the denom value to $.01, $.02, $.05, or $.10, with $.10 being the traditional option. When you think about it, it makes sense. The meter has to track every coin driven into the game. For that to work it must be able to increase the meter in whole numbers each time an event occurs. In this case every time a single credit is played the meter moves forward 2 denoms ($.20 = 2*$.10). The meters are basically hardwired odometers and they do not usually have fractional capabilities.

Likewise the denom may be set to $.01 for multi-denom games. A game with multi-denom capability gives the player options to choose the credit value they wish to play. As the meter must remain stable for proper tracking the lowest denom a number divisible into every available denom is the proper meter setting. Most casinos just make it a penny rather than do the math. At the end of the day it really only matters when you are looking at the slot analysis trying to figure out which denom does better. Remember the meter value will be what most systems show on the slot reporting side. Modern systems are starting to allow you to set each denom in a multi-denom game on its own meter setting, but this is far from being an industry standard at this point.

This all sounds confusing but really it is not. The credit value of the game is equal to what each credit is worth. The meter value of the game is equal to what the game meters in. The denom can loosely refer to either. The players at the game will use the credit amount, and that is how you should market it. But for slot analysis it is important to know which number your report is representing when you look at denom comparisons. Since most reports come from the system, it is most likely the metered value until someone manually changes it.

Chapter 12

Location Number,

The location number of most casino games in most casinos will be a 6 digit alphanumeric number that can be broken into three sections. The first two digits represent the section number. The second two digits the bank number. The last two represent the in bank placement. This number should change every time the game is moved. In order to ensure analysis is accurate every movement must be tracked. That way you can see how each area is doing.

Keeping location numbers logical and updated will also ensure employees on the floor have an easier time finding games. They will often use these numbers as sign posts for where they are, and where they are trying to reach. If your floor is currently not laid out in a logical manner, it is a time consuming yet simple affair of changing the system and the labels. It is well worth the time put in.

The section number is first and foremost, and usually a big distinguisher of how well the game will do. If your bar does poorly any games in this section will suffer in comparison to say games outside your buffet. Comparing games within a section will give you a better estimate of how that game is doing then comparing games from vastly differing sections. Also it is good to compare specific areas and sections averages to the overall casino average to track the ebb and flow of casino traffic. If a certain section is dropping in numbers you need to figure out why. Many casinos that have harsh winters will see sections near the doors drop in the winter times and rise in the summer time. Knowing this and getting ahead of it is vital to really controlling your floor. Also realizing that a bathroom is starting to smell and drive down numbers is pretty important.

I would suggest that when you are sectioning your casino you try to use a little logic to ensure you can really see how areas perform. Keep your non-smoking in one section, though if it is big enough use the second digit as a further indicator (i.e. if your smoking is AA, AB, AC then make your nonsmoking BA, BB, BC, etc.). Non-smoking is notoriously different from smoking sections. Keeping them sectioned apart means that you can easily pull up the different areas easily. Bars or cubby holes are also good to keep as their own section, or due to their size as sub sections created by the second digit. When you look at your floor think of the natural areas of distinction. Make each area a section. This will ensure accurate and logical distinctions in your slot analysis. It will even make more sense to your employees trying to use the numbers to find a machine.

The bank number is simply which bank within a section the game belongs to. A section should have several banks. Each bank should have its own number for ease of finding it. A weekly struggle, but a worthwhile one is ensure your bank numbers match a logical pattern on your floor. There is nothing more frustrating for your frontline staff looking for bank 04 to walk past bank 02, then bank 03 only to find bank 15. It will add unneeded frustration and extra time in them finding your customers. The bank numbers should be updated, and included on any maps you generate.

Bank placement number is where that game resides in the bank. Again this should follow a logical format. Pick a corner and always start your 01's there. It is simple as saying the numbers will work in a clockwise path starting at the one o'clock position. The method to your madness does not matter, as long as you are consistent. The importance of this number is not only so your employees can easily find the correct game once they locate the bank, but to ensure that when you run your numbers you know exactly where that game sits in the bank. When dealing with a six pack of games in a standard layout (non-circular or triangle or anything else, just a good old rectangle) machines with the numbers 02 and 05 will be in the center positions, while machines

01, 03, 04, and 06 will hold edge positions. The position of the game within the bank can and will usually effect the games play. Games in the inner positions usually doing slightly lower than the edge seats.

Keeping up on your location numbers and finding logical methods of assigning them is paramount not only for your slot analysis but also anyone trying to find a game on your floor. A little extra thought on your part, a little extra mindfulness with your techs, and your floor staff will thank you. A well laid out floor needs a well-designed location grid. Most casino floors neglect the finer touches in regards to this. Or when a big move comes they let it slide. But trust me, the attention to detail will be noticed by the boots on the ground.

Chapter 13

MFR and Description

The manufacturer of the game is simply the company that builds and sells the game. Sounds easy, it is easy. You will be dealing with multiple manufacturers in your career. It is important to learn which manufacturers are not only suited to your customers' style of play, but also which manufacturers' can keep their games running. There is nothing more frustrating than getting brand new pretty games that just keep breaking down, or your customers just cannot seem to find a use for.

Keeping good relationships with the quality manufacturers is vital to a lasting and updated casino floor. A good salesperson can help you find parts on outdated cabinets and even give you a heads up on coming promotions or chances for free conversions or discounted games. They can also give you a heads up if the company is getting ready to update everything and stop supporting current hardware. Early in my career I spoke to a slot director that walked into a floor that was just being updated with all new machines. She was excited to have all new only to find out that half of what her predecessor had bought and was being delivered was already on the stop support list for the manufacturers who had sold him their products. This was nothing he had done wrong. The salespeople had all assured him he was getting the newest and the greatest. What they failed to tell him was they were the newest and the greats for a few weeks more only. The new director then had to manage with these games because her predecessor had failed to maintain a good working relationship with his vendors or keep up on the industry.

Most floors prefer certain manufacturers. Trends in game cycles usually revolve around certain manufacturers. It is good know which games your customers like, and which ones they do not. Do they like innovation in bonus play, or do they just want free spins. Most manufacturers specialize in certain areas, even though their sales staff will probably tell you they do it all. It is also common for manufacturers to purchase each other. At that point all bets are off on what is getting supported and what is not.

This leads us to the label of description, which refers to the game's theme. Each manufacturer will have a cadre of themes to choose from all with their own options and settings to pick between. Themes are not only representative of pretty pictures and Hawai'ian deities to attract the customer, but also reflect a deeper math model that will hold customers' attention or not once they start playing. It is good to realize that your customers love dolphins and Egyptians, but do not be fooled that every ocean game is the same. Only the ones that offer the full experience will keep the players playing. Math models are usually split between volatility levels. Different players and different casino's preferring one style over the other. But again diversity is key. Ensure that even if your players love high volatility that you keep a few low volatility on the floor to ensure those customers going against your norm have something to play as well.

Which brings me to a very important point, just because your players love one manufacturer's specific theme and a set setting, do not think that you could fill an entire casino with that game and be just fine. You are attempting to build a diversified, visually appealing gaming floor upon which every player can find something to play, and hopefully something new to excite them. Make sure you are trying different manufacturers and several different themes. Make sure that you include performance guarantees in gaming contracts so that you can try out several different themes. And when you buy games and conversions let the salesperson pick a few, but make sure you get your say in what you want to try. It is your gaming floor after all. By diversifying themes and settings you will be making a big step in turning your slot floor into a beautiful amalgam of blinking lights, spinning screens, and the conglomeration of sounds that infest the casino world.

Part 5

Slot Analysis the Value Indicators

Here is the link:

https://drive.google.com/file/d/0B3H9gU1jTfZKSkNJWElF

U0dJc1E/view?usp=sharing

Ok get out the trusty link to the imaginary Lucky Draw's Casino Slot Analysis I gave you earlier. Let's dig into the numbers that will become your life for the rest of your career. I am really excited for those of you that are just now entering into the world of casino slot analysis. I just love to look at numbers and track the games. I spend nights after work playing around with pivot tables and sorting sections to get a feel for how each game is doing. The only thing I probably love more in life is using AutoCAD to actually design and redesign slot floors. The constant tinkering with scientific numbers in a way that require an artistic flare is really a joy to behold. One of the greatest moments you will ever have is when you finally work out the puzzle of a machine move and everything falls into place. And when you walk that floor and see people playing everything as designed, it is a moment of pride.

I call the numbers in this part the value indicators not because the other numbers do not have value. Instead these numbers we are about to go over help reveal value. They reveal the value of the games and sections they represent. They do this by showing us how much time, money, and energy players are willing to spend on the game you placed, the section you created, and the casino you built. These numbers allow us to judge if what we did was right. It gives us glimpses into how we can tinker with the floor to make it better. And you will tinker. You should tinker. Your floor needs to be a living organic entity.

Chapter 14

Daily Coin, Metered Coin In, and Coin Out

The Metered Coin In is an indicator of volume of play. It is most likely your marketing department's favorite number. They will use this number to build theoretic wins for the players, which will represent those players worth to the casino. But as important as coin in is, it is more important to remember that it is not an indicator of money made. But even so it is a vital number for proper slot analysis.

Every time a player hits spin it raises the coin in by the amount they played. Thus 10 spins of $1.00 will raise the coin in by $10.00, regardless of win or loss by the customer. What you are seeing is the player staying at the game and continuing to play. Low coin in means the player got bored and found somewhere else to play.

Taking the Metered Coin In and dividing it by the DOF you

will get the daily coin number which you will use to determine a

games daily play volume and the value of that game to your

customer base. A game that customers are willing to play for

hours and hours will have a high coin in to reflect that play. It is a

game they will want you to keep. The game itself should (if the

hold is true) be making you money over the long term even if it is

not making you large amounts in the short term. The constant

play will (read should) eventually even out the Win.

In the mock casino analysis that I created the average daily

coin of Lucky Draw Casino is about $1600. You can use this then

to judge games against the average. 208 games are below this

average and 92 games are above it. Northern Atlantic comes in

lowest with a daily coin of $160 and Golden Oil at a dollar comes

in highest with $9900. Section AB ranks best with $1921,

manufacturer Jouster Games with $4554, and finally the best

denom is $1.00s at $3965. Thus when looking at a game you want

to compare it not only to the overall average, but then to the

average of its section, its manufacturer, and its denom, only then will you get a real feel for how that game is doing in comparison to others like it.

If a game is doing well, but not as well as other like themes looking at the comparisons and contrasts will help you to decide how to get the most out of the game. Would it do better in a different section? Maybe with different settings? Bump it to a dollar or drop it to a nickel and see what happens. Looking at Golden Oil we have both dollar and nickel options. Perhaps moving one of the nickels up to a dollar will increase play, seeing how well the dollar game does. Be wary though as you may have just a few customers driving this dollar game's daily coin. Flooding the floor with them may alienate the nickel players and lower the overall average. Learn to balance each area and each setting to maximize profitability.

Coin Out, is the reverse of Coin In as it reflects the amount of money the machine paid over each spin. This number is not used as often to track anything specific other than the volatility of the game, and to correctly do some slot math. The coin out is not the amount the player took home. It is just the amount won over the course of playing. Thus if a player spins $1.50 and the machine pays back $.50 the coin out will be $.50, regardless that the amount won is less than the amount spun. The player's true balance is negative a $1.00, but the coin out is $.50.

Both the coin in and coin out are metered numbers that only go up. No matter what happens with the game the more it is played the more these two numbers should increase. At no point should you see the lifetime coin meters drop. They are strictly a record of the volume put in and won in the machine.

Chapter 15

Drop Numbers

The drop numbers shown on most slot analysis is broken down into Metered Bill Drop, Metered Coin Drop, Metered Voucher Drop, Metered Total Drop, Total Drop Variance, and Metered Adjusted Total Drop. The drop number reflects the amount of money found in the machine at the end of the day. Again this number is not the amount of money the machine made. It is only a reflection of the money inside the machine. If a player feeds several large bills into the game and cashes out the drop will be inflated. This can be caused by an attempt at money laundering at which case your title 31 should reflect it. It can simply be a superstitious player trying keep the machine thinking new players are coming and going.

The Metered Bill Drop is the amount of cash in the machine. With the modern TITO system this will be the bulk, if not the only, real cash in the machine. The system you use and the machine itself should be tracking how many of each type of bills is in the box and the order in which they should be found. There are screens you can get to on your gaming machine that you theoretically should be able to look at and see exactly what is in the bill box and in what order. When a bill goes in and does not credit, comparing this record with what is in the box will help you ensure that a bill was indeed lost and where.

Metered Voucher Drop is rather new to the gaming industry as it requires a TITO system to work. Most casinos now have TITO. It has spread like wildfire through the industry. This number represents every ticket that has been cycled through the game. The system and game should be able to show you the ticket amount, the ticket's unique ticket/voucher number, and the date and time it was entered. It is possible the date, time, and machine in which it was cashed out of can also be seen on game, if not the backend system will have it. The ability to track tickets makes finding thieves and ticket grazers easier. TITO has made it convenient for players to stay on property and change games without the need to hit a cashier every time they want to change it up.

Metered Coin Drop, much like Actual Fill is slowly becoming a thing of the past except with certain games kept for nostalgia purposes. This number represents the amount of coin the machine has inside of it. Every time a player drops a quarter the meter goes up. Few new games take coin, and for the bulk of games this number will always be zero.

As I am sure you have noticed all three of these numbers have the word metered in them, and added together they should equal the Total Metered Drop. The Total Metered Drop is all the money the machine thinks it has inside of the cash box. It is a representation of every transaction the machine recorded and reported to the system. At the end of the day though the drop team will come through take out all the money and the count team will count it. The count team's number will become the

Actual Drop, and be recorded with the system through some kind

of auditing function daily. Once this has occurred you will have

the Actual Adjusted Total Drop, which will be the verified Actual

Drop.

The difference between the Total Metered and Adjusted

Drop is known as the Total Drop Variance or just the variance.

The variance should always be reported on your slot analysis and

a multitude of variances should be investigated. The modern

gaming system of machine, back end system, and drop/count

teams should really have no problem matching up even large

amounts of transactions as 90% of it is automated.

Variances happen, but the frequency and amount of each

variance should be closely watched by your audit staff. As a

casino manager you should also feel responsible for keeping a

close eye on discrepancies. If it is the same machine over and

over, checking that the machine is metering correctly or having

surveillance keep an eye on the game is just due diligence of protecting your casino's assets.

Daniel Hansen

Chapter 16

Actual Attendant Payouts and Vouchers Issued

Vouchers Issued is the total of all the vouchers the
machine printed. Each and every successful cash out will be
reflected in this number. This number is newer in that tickets
have been able to print in machines for decades now, but the use
of TITO has made it much more secure. Now each ticket that
comes out of a machine with a back end system has a ticket
number and a validation code through the system and often a bar
code for ease of cashing. No longer must we keep boxes of
carbon copies to match tickets out of the machine. The back end
system tracks each ticket and where it goes. The ability to track
tickets has made finding thieves, ticket grazers, and just plain lost
and damaged tickets that much easier. It has revolutionized
gaming. It has improved what a casino floor worker can do to

ensure they are helping customers and protecting the casino's

assets at the same time.

Actual Attendant Payouts represent any time the

customer is paid by an attendant instead of through a ticket.

These range from normal daily occurrences to dramatic

exceptions.

At times the employee will be Creating Tickets known as a

Pouch Pay. Creating a ticket should always be the last thing

considered. It is usually caused when the machine malfunctions

and goes into a critical unrecoverable error. These pays are not

initiated by the machine, but by the employee. Supervisors

should be present for and approve all ticket creations. Pouch Pays

are handled at the machine, usually through the back end

system's card reader. The same process done at a computer like

an FJP machine is also possible (usually referred to as a "ticket

creation" rather than a pouch pay). You will need the machine's

information to complete the transaction, again a supervisor

should be available. Both of these will be recorded under

Attendant Payouts, and assigned to the machine and tracked.

Now Damaged Tickets or a Ticket did not Print should not require a true attendant pay as the machine can track what the damaged or missing ticket's information is and the process can be handled through the cage system. The missing ticket will be voided or "cashed," this is a much safer method as you know there was a ticket and if the real ticket does show up the system will notify you. These will not be tracked as an Attendant Payout, but as a voucher pay at the machine, and a damaged ticket at the cage.

Handpays are similar to the above issues, but the machine realizes there is an error and initiates the event. These are recorded as Attendant Payouts. If the machine jams up, runs out of paper or some other event occurs causing the machine to malfunction during the cash out and it realize that it malfunctioned then it will lock up and initiate the handpay. These events should notify the employee if they will require a supervisor present or not. Either way it will be recorded as an Attendant

Payout and reflected in this area for your analysis.

Jackpots requiring processing will also be found in this area. This will most likely be your highest frequency and largest amounts in this section. Everybody loves a good jackpot. I often check this area for weekend totals so that I can flaunt how much the casino paid out in wins. It is important to remember that most machines are set up at the taxable limit of $1200.00 for lock up. So this line will grow quickly if a machine is hitting. Also remember that according to the IRS that is a "single win" amount, not a single spin amount. Free spins unless counted as different wins will add together to reach the limit. Many people falsely believe this only applies to progressive jackpots, but sadly, no. It applies to all big wins.

There is a trend currently in casinos to lower this from $1200 to increase the perception of wins. It will also increase the amount of time each customer is touched by an employee. With a setting of say $600, the employees get to celebrate more wins, and customers will see that. Further, more customers will be celebrated and have that "I won" experience so sought after on the casino floor. Of course this requires on the ball staff, and quick ability to process the win. You want to ensure an attempt to celebrate does not turn into many different frustrated customers waiting to get paid. A customer waiting to get paid is a customer not playing the game.

A machine with a high coin in and low win will often have a large jackpot that is skewing its results, so make sure you pay attention to Attendant Payouts to ensure that you are properly valuing the game. Also use this area to track employees that may be handling a lot of ticket creations, as they should be done rarely and with good reason. Basic slot accounting will combine all these areas. Drilling down into the reports should allow you to separate one from the other, and then start to track who is processing what. Because the area involves human error and large sums of money trusted in the hands of individuals it is also the weakest part of the system and most open to abuse. Keeping an eye on this area is vital to protecting your casino's assets, so keep an eye out.

For slot analysis this area is also one of the most likely to cause a large skew in your numbers. A game that has been going like gang busters could take a huge dive in both the Win and Hold with a single large jackpot to sink the numbers. Be sure to look at a game's numbers both with and without the jackpot to gauge its real worth. The last thing you want to do is see a negative Net Win and out of reactionary behavior dump a machine that just took a jackpot hit and should be getting back up to speed in no time. For example in the Luck Draw Casino machine BA0216 had some pretty extreme jackpot's going on. They killed the games Win (which would have been $386 a day without the jackpots). It is always good to double check your numbers, and see what is affecting the overall analysis. Seeing this you should start asking what caused the high jackpots and if it is accurate. There could be many reasons valid and shady that might cause this.

Chapter 17

Win and Average Win per Unit per Day,

The game's Win. Finally the number that represents the amount of money you made off the game. The win is calculated by taking the drop and minus out the payouts. It should in theory have a correlation with the Coin In because of the assigned par percentage. But with the random nature of games, this will be in a constant state of flux. The shorter the duration you make your analysis the more varied it will be and the less the two will correlate.

Looking at the Lucky Draw Casino Analysis again we can see our average is $135. Further we can tell that that Fire's 7 sets at the low end with a negative $4,000 and the dollar Golden Oil is top with $940. Further, section HD has the high of $270, manufacturer Legacy Games at $154, and the best Denom is dollars at about $300. Let's compare this to the coin in numbers if you recall they were, Northern Atlantic $160 and Golden Oil $9900, section AB $1921, manufacturer Jouster Games $4554, and denom $1.00s at $3965. So we have some overlap in the areas of our Golden Oil taking both top coin in and top win, and dollars also taking both top spots. Looking at this we may need a few more dollar games, and a phone call to the sales rep to see what they have similar to Golden Oil for purchase.

On your own try the numbers with removing the highest and lowest 5 games. Do your numbers go up or down? And why, why do you think the average would go up due to this removal? The answer is simply that big jackpot is dragging down all the numbers. Jackpots that grow for long periods of time have that effect on short term slot analysis, and skew how things go in the short term. Our analysis is only 19 days, so this kind of irregularity and wide fluctuation is common. To even look deeper, look at the

Columbian Lady at CA1412. It has a mid-level slightly below house average coin in but the win is well over house at $357. Finding these irregularities and seeing what is going on at the game level is an important part of the analysis. Mainly because this game is making a good amount of money with a low hold percentage but is only getting average play. Once this hold percentage starts to even out we should see the game's win drop to a more average level. The game is over holding. Be excited for the moment, but understand things will right themselves over time.

Chapter 18

Hold Percentage and Occupancy Percentage

The hold percentage is the percentage the game should try to keep from each spin on average. It has an inverse relationship with the setting the techs will set known as the Par Percentage. The Par is the amount of money the machine should try to give back from each spin to the customers. For an example if the techs set the par at 88% then the hold should be 12%. Now this is a theoretical hold seeing as the game is random, and only over time will it be able to reach its desired hold. The shorter period you run numbers on the more off the hold percentage will be from its theoretical hold. You can figure your actual hold percentage also using the simple formula of win/coin in. There are actually several different formulas used to reach the hold, but this is the most common, and most likely the one your system will use. A few of the other formulas (some based off table games) will get varying numbers, so stay consistent when comparing.

Through the par the hold then is settable. Through it you loosen or tighten the game. Most casinos have a set process in determining what a game's hold percentage should be. The industry tradition is that dollars are the loosest and pennies are the tightest, with participation and leased games being on the tight end of the spectrum. I fully support tightening up participation and especially leased games. These games should not share all the benefits that house games have. Players should play these games because they are drawn to them, not because they are loose. It is important to remember your distinction between games you own and games you do not, and finding ways to draw players to games you own should be part of your strategy.

Breaking down games by denom to ensure that only the "big" players get the loose games is traditional, but it is my personal belief it is outdated. I play quarter games, single line, with a max bet of $.75. I gamble with people who play penny games with a max bet of $4.00. Now which of us is a big player? Traditional casinos would say me. Further the bulk of your players are going to be penny players, and a player is really playing for experience. They know they might not win. Heck they know they probably will not win. But they do want time on device. Let's face it giving the bulk of your customers an 88% par is not giving them time on device. Heck it is barely giving them a chance to set down and think about the game.

By flattening the denom based hold percentage and upping your floor's overall looseness you will increase players' time on device and increase their satisfaction as a gambler. Increased satisfaction will drive more play and more trips. In my experience running casino floors I know two things: One, most of those reading this will ignore it because it flies in the face of traditional thinking. And two, it works, it works very-very well.

A note on a final metric that many casinos should be

looking at and that is occupancy percentage. By looking at the occupancy percentage you will be better prepared to schedule employees as required for the casino's needs and ensure that you know when your busiest times happen. You will also be able to get a baseline that allows you to very easily and in the moment track the success of promotions and events. By looking at how many players are usually there on a Monday you can tell if your Monday promo is increasing this number or not. Occupancy percentage is a great tool, and it can be tracked in real time very easily with modern back end systems.

Do not assume though that a high or low occupancy equates to a higher win. You would rather have four $5,000.00 a trip players than 500 $5.00 a trip players. Many casinos make this mistake with events. Events almost always cause the win to drop. Fewer "real" gamblers come out and play when packed. Instead you have a multitude of low level players that need more assistance and babysitting. Events are great to introduce your property to new guests. They are vital to a healthy casino. They should not be relied on to drive business though. Traditionally

they drive away the business you want for a night.

Daniel Hansen

Part 6

Let's Play with the Numbers

Now that we have an understanding what all the numbers

mean, it is time to play around with our numbers to ensure we

have a proper understanding of how to use the excel document to

see what we are looking at. We do this by going back into our

excel sheet and doing some sorting and some formulas. You will

need to download the document so that you can edit, editing will

be key.

Here is the link:

https://drive.google.com/file/d/0B3H9gU1jTfZKSkNJWElF

U0dJc1E/view?usp=sharing

First open the Cash Draw Casino excel sheet and go to the

slot report work sheet. The tabs are at the bottom of the screen.

Work sheets are individual pages within the document and the

document as a whole is called a workbook. Once you are in the

Slot Report Worksheet you can select column I for coin in (rows

go side to side and are numbered, columns go up and down and

are lettered, and cells are the individual boxes). Once you have

highlighted the entire column by selecting the letter you can sort

from highest to lowest. You should see asset number 70,000 with

a coin in of $9914.95 as the top machine. You can do this sort for

any and all columns. The top ten machines are doing well over

house average. Take a look at the top ten games and get a feel

for about what our top performers are doing. Now scroll to the

bottom and look at the bottom ten. What similarities do all of the

bottom performers have in common? Why do you think this is? If

it is a bank or location concern and this was a real world scenario

you would want to actually walk down and look at the bank. A

machine caught in a cold air draft might just need moved.

Now that you know how to sort it, it is time to figure out

what is average about the numbers we value as good or bad in

the games. I have already created an Averages worksheet so you

can look at it and see that we have an average of $1596.27. For

this and most standard averages we will be using the mean

average, which in excel is =Average(desired cells). But let's see if

you can create your own average line. For this I have a blank

table ready for you to fill in. On your slot analysis you can enter

sums and averages on the document with all the information, but

I prefer a second work sheet for ease of use and to keep down the

clutter.

Click on the D9 cell and type in =Average(now without

leaving the cell click back to the slot report worksheet and choose

the daily coin in column and close the formula with). Your cell

should show the $1596.27 and the formula line should read:

=AVERAGE('LUCKY DRAW CASINO SLOT REPORT'!I:I). Now you

have your daily coin average and can gauge the good and bad coin

in machines. Go back to the report page and look at those games

above and below the average. You can see which games the

customers spend the most time on. The top performers are the games they dump the most money into. To ensure you have a capable understanding of this simple formula, now fill in the rest of the averages cells and ensure they match mine. You are doing great.

Let's now compare average win by our lowest performer. You have created your averages column and so you know that your average per unit win is $135.21. Go back to the report page and pick column R or per unit. Ensure that when you click the R it highlights the entire column. Sort lowest to highest (the opposite of last time), and you will find the lowest games is 80,001. Your win will be crazy low, actually in the negative, but why? The average coin in is a little below house average, but not ridiculously low and even your drop is in the average range. But look at the attendant pay out column and you will find our answer. Remember this area includes jackpots and it is most likely that the $80,000 comes from that. You can see here that the jackpot is actually bringing your numbers way down.

Let's see exactly what the win would be if there was no jackpot? For this formula you will be clicking cells and not entire columns. To get your Win you are going to want to add (Metered Cash Drop + Metered Voucher Drop) – (vouchers out + Attendant Pay Outs). Normally the second part would look like (Vouchers Out + Attendant Pay Outs) but seeing as we are removing the jackpot amounts remove the Attendant Pay Outs, just remove the number. So I will give you the formula but I suggest as you create it and experiment with picking cells instead of typing in the cell name it will make it all sink in a little better. Pick any empty cell and type in =sum((K300+L300)-(P300)) this will give you the win without the jackpot. The standard win formula will instead look like =sum((K+L)-(O+P)).

Side note you can also take the theoretical hold (what it was set at), instead of the actual hold and multiply it by coin in. You will get what the win should be (using actual hold is another way to calculate win).

For our Win number you should see $7,345.00. This is the

full win for the entire DOF. To get the per unit go to the cell beside the one you are in and type in =sum(now click the cell you just created and put in the division sign and choose the DOF cell, if done correctly you will see a win of $386.58. As you can see without that large jackpot this game's win is actually extremely high. Of course the machine did hit a jackpot or jackpots that currently cost you $80,000. It will be good to watch the game and ensure that more jackpots do not keep cutting into your profits. I would take another step and ask the Cashier or Audit staff if a single large jackpot hit on this machine, or if it is a series of small jackpots. There is also the danger that attendants are creating tickets here or somehow using this machine to steal. My advice red flag it. Do not freak out. But investigate.

Now let's look at the numbers added together and summed up. A quick note, a sum of your hold is kind of useless, so I never bother to create it. Sums of percentages do not really tell you much, and this number is a percentage. But let's say you want to be able to tell customers how much you have been paying off in jackpots. So you will need a total sum of the Attendant Payouts. Now I know the Attendant Payout number will include handpays and such, but their addition should be minimal so you can feel safe in claiming that 99% of what is here are jackpots. Go back to the average page and you will see that I have already created a sum line. But again I have left a blank line for sums for you to fill out. First go to the jackpot cell and choose it. Now type in =sum(and without leaving the cell go back to the reports page and choose the jackpot column. Close the formula with a) and you are ready to go. Your jackpot sum should read =SUM('LUCKY DRAW CASINO SLOT REPORT'!O:O) in the formula line and in the cell it should equate to $153,249.35. Not a bad payout for such a small casino and a short period of time. Now that you understand how to create the sums line start filling in all the boxes. Ensure they match my numbers in my own table.

The summation will give you a solid grasp on what your casino did for the entire time period, and/or what it does in total for an entire day. The most useful part of this is the win and per unit line. Looking at these cells you will see that the win is $768,107.71 and the per unit is $40,426.72. This indicates that the casino made gross about $770,000 in the 19 days we ran the analysis for and it averages about $40,000 a day.

Of course seeing as the per unit is the total win divided by the DOF the number is a bit oversimplified. I say this because it treats every day equally, but that is not true. Most casinos have busy days and slow days. The weekends are traditionally going to make the bulk of your revenue. If you poll just a single Friday the numbers should come in higher than the per unit average you run over a long period of time. Once you get more comfortable in your analysis career, I would suggest you look at specific days versus specific days. By this I mean look at event Fridays against nonevent Fridays. Look at Christmas 2014 versus Christmas 2015, because in this way you will start to be able to gauge how specific days and events do against other days that should be similar if not for the event or holiday.

Let's say you are just wondering how an area is doing but

do not want to do all the formulas and work. It is just a quick

wonder. Let's sort the Report page by Location, the top bank

should be AA01 and has nine games on the bank. Go to the daily

coin in column and highlight from AA0101 to AA0109, this is

column I and rows 2 to 10. Once you have them highlighted look

at the bottom right side of the document in the green bar and you

should see a row of Average, Count, and Sum. This is the quick

look at these figures for just the cells you have selected. It is a

good way to make a quick check before doing anything else, or to

just answer a quick question without filling in all the formulas.

Now let's say you want to look at a specific grouping, and

get the totals for each group quick and easy. I have done this for

you in the Section, Manufacturer, and Denom Averages pages. I

used the quick and easy method of copying my reports page and

pasting it in a blank worksheet. After that you sort by the column

you are going to want as your main subject. So if you want the

sums and averages of all the denoms you sort by denom. Now go

to the tabs at the top of the page and choose the Data column and find the Subtotal option. Click and a wizard should pop up, choose, "at each change in" "denom" and then either "average" or "sum" which ever you want, then click the boxes of all the columns you are going to want values for. Hit apply and Excel does all the work. You now have "−" signs at the top left side of the table, click − 2 and the table should fold down to just the subtotals. Use the blank worksheet I have provided to try this and then check it versus the ones provided to ensure that you are on the right path.

Lastly I would like you to go into the pivot table worksheet I created. I already have the pivot table started all you need to do is click on the table and the right side will be populated with choices. Pivot tables are a bit more complex. You will want to really take some time and play around with it. For now ensure that when you put different things to evaluate into the separate areas of the pivot table go into "value field settings" and choose if you want averages, sums, or anything else. The default setting is "count" which gets annoying as you make multiple changes quickly. Honestly you almost never use "count."

As a quick tutorial you need to put the information you want in the value box. Change it how you want the value field settings. In this test table I have Averages of Daily Coin. Now you can have either the row or the column box empty You will need something in at least one box to differentiate the values. I have under rows denom, and under columns section. This means that as you look at the table from left to right you have average daily coin by section and top to bottom you have average daily coin by denom. The beauty of the table is not only that it is quick but that you can see that pennies in section AA make a different average than dollars in BB. My suggestion is that you first make sure you are comfortable with the standard tables and cells. As you grow more confident you start playing around with pivot tables. Pivot tables make analysis much quicker and easier once you understand them. Being able to use them is really a skill that makes life much easier.

Part 7

The End of the Line

I have been in this industry for soon to be decades (yes plural I am getting old) now. That is crazy to even consider. Especially when I have loved almost every moment of it. How many people can work in an industry for so long and still love every moment? I have made friendships through networking that will last the rest of my life. I owe special thanks to people like Bert Vega from Prairie Bend in Kansas and Tim Yovanovich from Coeur d'Alene Casino in Idaho. When it comes to slot analysis these two men really emphasis two paths a friendship can take. They have both taught me a lot.

When I met Bert it was while I was bragging to Harrah's

executives that they should visit my casino (a small north Idaho casino) as it was the greatest casino in the world. I rather unshyly informed them that every other casino hoped to one day reach our level, but their hopes were in vain. Bert thought I was hilarious. I still think the reaction from the Harrah's crowd was priceless. We hit off a great and lasting friendship. Bert is a slot analysis expert. Any question I have about how a game is doing anywhere in the world I call Bert. More than an expert he is someone I connect with. He is someone I can have long conversations with about changing denoms. If you should let them be multi-game. We argue hold percentages and what color a base should be. And at the same time we can set back and joke about life. He is just an expert in our field and if you ever see him at a trade show tell him Dan Hansen said howdy.

Tim on the other hand was a Cabinet Maker turned Bench Tech when I first met him. I have watched him learn both excel and slot analysis. Our relationship has grown from me telling him how to map machines to him bringing new maps for layouts for me to look at and in-depth slot reports he has created. We have had more conversations about how games and sections are doing then probably any other people I know. I have a great amount of respect for Tim and his ability to take what he has been taught and turn it into something greater. If he remembers that the hold percentage is the win divided by the coin in, he will lose fewer arguments. But heck, excel does most of the work for us anymore.

My point in discussing these two great people is that you will need to network. No casino or analyst should be going it alone. I can guarantee that you are going to run into a problem that your vendors will tell you, "That has never happened before." And a few emails and phone calls later you will discover that it is happening everywhere. Whether the vendors lie, or just do not bother to communicate in house, I have never cared. What I do care about is solving issues and getting new ideas. Both of which networking will help with. You will have questions as you learn, and a few good friends are never a bad idea.

Another good idea is start to walk your floor if you are not doing it regularly. I cannot stress enough that you learn your floor. Going out to walk amongst the customers and employees both on your slow days and busy nights is necessary to really being able to analysis what is going on. Getting a feel for what is out there and what may or may not be effecting a games playability will ensure that once you do start looking at the accounting side you have a full picture. It is important to remember that change should be geared toward making things improved not making things different, and knowing your floor will cut back on unnecessary experiments.

Not only is it educational but it is fun. There is nothing better than designing, mapping, and building a slot floor and then walking it. To see what was in your head and on a flat computer screen come to life in 3D blinking lights and spinning screens is an amazing experience. Walking that floor, seeing the reality. From the log jams you will need to adjust to the surprising 'meadows' you never planned. All of it comes together like a well thought out sculpture. That is how you should think of your floor an organic, living, breathing, and hopefully interactive sculpture. I can promise you, that you will never be happy with all the parts of it. Live with each change for a time, see what it does, then adjust.

Every machine move and change should be a mix of analysis and beauty, concentrating on one or the other for too long will degrade your floor. The analysis informs the final result. More importantly it informs any adjustments that come later.

I wish you the greatest luck in playing with your slot numbers and growing your floor into a thing of beauty. I hope you find as much joy in this business as I have.

Quyanaqpak,

dhansen

ABOUT THE AUTHOR

Daniel Hansen started working in Indian Gaming in September of 1997 at a native casino, and he spent his entire adult life learning everything he could about how the industry works and actively managing staff, which he still does as a Casino Executive. He is an enrolled member of the Village of Kotzebue and a shareholder of NANA Corp. His background allows him to see Native Casinos through the eyes of a businessman, a lawyer, a philosopher, and still remember true success does not necessarily come just with a bigger bottom line, but an empowered tribal membership and an improved community. He firmly believes in Servant Leadership, and only by empowering others will he find success in this life.

Basically he is super awesome...

Made in United States
North Haven, CT
18 October 2024

59138212R00088